Reclaim.

A Collection of Poetry and Essays

1

For Us.

For those of us who are seen and unseen.

For my Mom

My sisters

My Nana

My Aunties

My Family.

For Thelma

Alvin

Yvonne

Jo Mason

And Mary.

For every Black Woman in Charlottesville that showed me the way

Corrected me

Loved me

And held me up.

For Us.

I want to start by saying that this was not supposed to happen. I had no real intention of writing a book. I put it off over and over again, because I didn't think that it was my place to discuss the matters of misogyny, erasure, and activism in my town. I thought that it was normal for people to silence me as a young person, simply because I was a young Black woman. I took the backseat on my own efforts because I thought no one was listening. I woke up one day, and Charlottesville had become a hashtag, but missing in the national narrative was all of the hard work of Black women that had been going on for decades in this city. And I asked myself, how did we, Black women, become displaced from something we built? How did my name and face get lost from something that I wrote?

I came to the realization that people had been hearing my words all across the country, but crediting Black women on major platforms is not particularly profitable unless it is trending.

It is easier to just speak about the notion of respecting and protecting Black women, but the commitment to the act of amplification is seldom made.

Ideas that I conveyed through my metaphoric pen onto a single letter to the editor and city officials, rapidly caught fire and attention as it awakened a dormant community of activists and organizers right before my eyes. The work in Charlottesville was already there, we knew what needed to be done to organize around the removal of these racist statues, and we did just that.

A catalyst. In the spring of 2016, I did something that scared me, but something that I knew needed to be done. I wrote the petition, a letter to the editor and city council, calling for the removal of the Lee statue and the renaming of the park, formerly known as Lee Park. I was 15.

In this collection of journal entries, iPhone notes, and essays I will reclaim the my work, my time, and my energy. We, as people, perpetually fail to cite Black Women. It seems that it is so much easier to co-opt the words and work of Black women, instead of being honest that it was them who started it. It is so much easier to center one's self in someone else's work than just joining in and taking their leadership. Now, it's 2019, and not much has changed. Black women are still being asked for free intellectual and emotional labor. Many still enjoy the optics of bringing Black women to their tables, tokenizing them, and then taking their ideas. As activism is increasingly trendy, Black people and Black needs are still sidelined. Black women remain the political and social mules of this country. However, what I can say, I have never been more proud to be a Black Woman. Despite being told for years that I am too loud, too assertive, and bossy; despite being erased from an initiative that I catalyzed with my own writing; and despite being told that I am not going to make it, I am here to say that I am. I am doing all of the things that I

have been conditioned to believe that I couldn't.

I am reclaiming my work, my time, and my space.

I belong here.

I deserve to be here.

And Damn,

 I am proud to be a Black Woman.

If you heard the story of Charlottesville, the tiki torches, and the

nazis marching on the grounds of UVA,

But you didn't hear about the tireless work of Black women that

sparked the true change that came as a result,

You heard it wrong.

These are my words of struggle, triumph, and affirmation.

Purpose

"More of the movement, less of myself."
-Zyahna

I cannot say it enough,
That I am who I am because of the pressure of my village
And the Molding of my experiences.

All of my success can be equally attributed to both, respectively.
While I share my life and vibrations
My only plea is that we enlighten and share
Even when we are not willingly being heard.

Something is better than nothing.
If only two gather in the presence and under the precedent of the movement
A fire has been ignited.

December 17th, 2017.
(Writing in my Sweet Spot to the noise of reality TV)

I. Space

The way that we maneuver through space is so contingent upon the ways that we choose to identify. My belief is beyond levels of comfort, our identity also guides our moral compass of sorts that tells us when spaces are not for us. When I authored the petition to Charlottesville City Council back in the Spring of 2016, I was fully aware that a park beneath the shadow of a Confederate general was not the place for me. This was not a space where I could be myself, without being reminded of the historical trauma that I carry with me everyday. I was also fully aware that Charlottesville, VA, Confederate land, was home, but mostly in a physical sense. This was home; but this was also the place where I was first called a nigger at my rather, elite private school located just outside of town. This was the place where the only day of the week that I was surrounded by people of skin complexions similar to mine, was Sunday. I grew up and gained my voice in a Black church, on the Black side of town. Stockings,

13

usher gloves, hymnals, and all. I felt joy in this space, on Sundays and then only again in my house, and in the embrace of my mother, grandmother, and aunties. It was in these spaces where I could recharge and breathe. These spaces were safe havens from being the spectacle. The spaces where I could feel.

Charlottesville has always been divided. In this place, 52% of the people who lived here were enslaved until the Confederates lost the civil war. This city has always been separated by train tracks. It is really no coincidence that Summer 2017 happened here. People ask how and why, but it is simple. This place is built on White Supremacy and division. The way that the serpentine walls that surround the lawn of Thomas Jefferson's prestigious university, was used to silence the whispers and cries of people who look like me, is the same way that I feel the hand of institutions gripping the necks of my peers so that they cannot advocate for their own upward mobility. The concept of borders and walls is what can be found at the root of this progressive town. This is the place where after nearly seven years, there are still no answers for the disappearance of Sage Smith, a transgender Black woman, yet the cases of local white college students have garnered national coverage. Many argue that those in power did not stop what was to come here because they were not equipped with the resources to do so; but just like many other things, why fix something that is not broken? Black people have been gradually pushed out of this town for decades. From urban renewal to gentrification, we have been told over and over again that this place is not for us.

No one has protected us from the uprooting of our homes. No one has protected us from the excessive policing and patrolling of our neighborhoods. We protect us. We make space for us. We always will protect us. That was no different on August

12th, 2017, and it still remains true today. We will always protect

us. I will always protect us, all of us.

Ghana in April

I am healing. The traumatic reality of white supremacy and the oppression of Black lives is not an easy one to live with. When I was at my lowest, it was the faith that others held in me and for me, that kept me pushing. Not for reasons of pride or even further accomplishment; but it was love. Love in the midst of the struggle, love in the midst of hate. Love from the church, and the same agape love from those with no desire for religious affiliation. All of that love.

Love lifted me. Truly it was love that picked me up and pushed me forward when I convinced myself that I could no longer stand.

I was in denial. I knew that the road to justice was going to be full of turns, hurdles, violence, and indifference. However, I did underestimate our ability to self-destruct our own side of the movement. I blindly believed that we could all get on the same

17

page, because after all, we were activists with the common goal of equity for black lives.

I was wrong. While I found myself having a very unplanned involvement in this movement for racial justice, I underestimated the presence of toxic egos who would use the fight against white Supremacy as an opportunity to capitalize and push their political agendas and careers.

I was told by a teacher that "we have to learn how to separate people from their politics." I went with his claim for a while, because it seemed reasonable. Now, as I reflect on this conversation, I cannot simply accept this. Too often, we want to talk about redeeming qualities of individuals. That is wrong. Why do we always have to work to see the good in those that utilize systems of racial inequality to perpetuate inequity and oppression? Why must we be told to excuse their behavior? Why are we always told how we should express our outrage, by those who couldn't even begin to fathom the pain in our experiences?

Just when I began to grasp the concept of Self Care, my life was changed forever. It was 2016, and Solange dropped one of the biggest albums of the year. "A Seat at the Table" was so powerful that it introduced broad concepts that applied to my life in more ways than one. Even the youngin' I was at the time, Just finally turning the page of Self Care and Self Love, it began to all make sense. I was so consumed with wanting to care for myself, meditate, and find happiness in my time alone. No one quite understood it, but it made feel so empowered and in control of my being when I was alone and grinding and resting.

So, it was in Ghana, in April, that I made this realization. I needed to be here, and I'm thankful that I've been welcomed with open arms.

Ghana.
May 2018.

Trayvon

       I was 12 when I organized my first demonstration. I stood on the corner of Main Street directly in front of the Federal Courthouse building in Charlottesville. Up to that point, I was only a 12 year old that I knew was following every detail of the of the trial. I attempted to to discuss the events of the trial with everyone that I knew. Mainly because I wanted everyone to tell me that it was going to be okay. I wanted reassurance from those around me. I longed for the general consensus to be that he was guilty beyond a reasonable doubt.

       It turned out that it didn't matter. As deliberation stalled, I had this internal understanding that Justice was not going to be served. However, that did not lessen the blow when the verdict was officially announced. It still felt like a stab in the heart. I kept asking myself, how did we get here? How did the happy feelings and tears of joy that flowed on election night of 08', turn into screams of terrified mothers sobbing for Trayvon and the existence of their own black sons?

       I sat in my Grandmother's house, slouched in the brown chair that was placed in the corner of the living room under the lamp, and I was paralyzed. It's like my body shut down, and the words refused to roll off my tongue. After a few minutes of time

21

standing still, I walked out of the house and onto the porch. I thought maybe something would be different. It wasn't. I came back inside and went back to my seat. I watched CNN, where protesters had taken the streets. I kept saying how I wished that I was there because I was not sure how to begin processing this. I wanted to unpack this. I wanted to understand why the elders around, warned me not to get my hopes up. I wanted to put together eloquent thoughts and make a moving social media post as a way to start processing this. I couldn't. I was hurt. This was a pain that I'd never felt before. This pain was worse than rejection; worse than isolation. This pain was even worse than the pain of a broken family. This was the pain of realizing that there was no one to protect us. There still is no one to protect us. The epiphany that it could have been any of us.

"What happened to Trayvon was so wrong that they normalized

it until it felt right."

-Zyahna Bryant, diary entry (2014)

The Summer of the Blue Dashiki

The days are long
As I check Instagram for the most recent indictment
Or lack thereof
Or shooting
I carry Assata in my backpack to and from work
As if my chances of being revolutionary
Are that great
As I assume my position
As an intern
In a public office
Of an oppressive government
In an oppressed city
Just teetering on the brink of Trump's
Amerikkka.

My hair curls just right
I've become more fond of denman brushes than combs.
Being Carefree is trendy.
I don't look out of place wearing my Dashiki in the mall.
The country is high off of blackness.
Black people are low
From lack of compensation
For the bits and pieces
Being removed
Misused
And misconstrued
But
It's ours

Right?

I got up the next morning
 that was my act of resistance.
When my feet hit the floor
Power flowed through veins like an unsettled river.
I felt strong.
I had Another opportunity to wrestle with my demons
And plant myself in the unknown.

Hot July

And Malcolm speaks to me in my dreams

And on the street

We gathered on

Market

To be exact.

Right outside of the Police Station

With a permit

No harm

Just posters

And small black children with popsicle stains on their shirts

And sharpie all over their hands

They enjoyed the screaming

Some say they know not what they are screaming for

But I say they are very much alive.

I couldn't imagine the movement without the 10 year olds.

The ones that ask the most questions.

Everywhere That I go

I fold back a new layer of myself

And leave a piece of me there.

Spain.

April 2016.

I have learned to live in a mindset driven by Carpe Diem! That goes specifically for opportunity. When opportunities come knocking, I take them. I've spent a lot my very early childhood being afraid to express whatever it was that I wanted to say. As I reached middle school, I began to just go for whatever was in my reach. When it comes to academics, my thirst for learning is unwavering and has been that way since I was in my first years of my education at a local private school. Those around me have pushed me. My grandmother has always signed me up for whatever she saw was available. She always reminded me that she knew that I would not like or enjoy everything. However, she made it the business of her and my mother to make sure that many doors were unlocked for me, my cousins, and my sisters. They knew that we would have to watch the doors open and decide which path we wanted to take on our own. And we did.

They have supported us every step of the way. So, when people

ask how I became this way, they are the answer.

Here's to Openness and transparency.

And being upfront.

And Saying everything you mean to say

Without masking it with humor.

1/1/2018

Tomorrow.

Take me to tomorrow.

Perhaps better things await.

And there I will find myself.

II. Identity

I loathe boxes, stereotypes, and boundaries that are created to place limits on my Freedom. I cannot recall the last time I learned something from an easy journey, or the last time I saw my father either without a bottle in his hand, or with his presence being free from bars and bullet-proof glass; but, what I do know is that all of this has shaped me to live unconventionally and fight radically. When I wake up in the morning, many things go through my mind, including the nightmares of future downfalls and failures, but as my spine unfolds and my chest rises toward the ceiling, I remind myself that today, I must take a side.

Arms locked, humming the melodies of battle songs first whispered by my ancestors, we were confronted by a looming cloud of uncertainty that consumed the streets of Charlottesville in the thick of Summer. Hands folded, heads bowed, voices trembling, I embraced my comrades for what I thought could have been the last time. "Which side are you on?" I asked myself, as the reverend reached the benediction. Palms sweaty, clocks ticking, feet marching, it was now or never. Everything was still. My eyes flooded with tears and I felt the distant voice of my father reminding me that I was his Freedom Fighter. Radical Love. The same love that gets me through the daily battle of forgiving him for his absence in my life or the violence that he brought against my being is the same love that supported me and kept me on the early morning of the 12th of August. I was no longer in the fetal position covering my head in a corner as my mother crouched over me, shielding me as he swung the bat against our skulls. This time I was in the front and she was behind me. Radical growth.

Radically I stood with a collective force against the ugliness that lurks beneath the surface of our comfortable illusion of this city. But radical, I am, just by existing, alone. Because my Blackness is radical enough to be forgotten on that day and all of the days that have passed and that are to come. Radical because decolonizing and dismantling systems of oppression is far from sexy and it is not the easiest concept to market. Radical because I will never pass a paper bag test, radical because media limits my thoughts to rage and anger that will drive up their ratings. Radical because I hold space and serve as a barrier to business as usual when justice is absent.

I am radical not because I choose to be, but because I have to be. The same way that I extended radical forgiveness to my father to liberate myself is the same way that I seek to emancipate myself from the socioeconomic and racial boxes that force me into political imprisonment. Radical is my existence, just as much as it is my nature of Survival.

We never really know who

We are

Until we have to.

Black Women Superhero-ism

Course Correction

Blinds us

Into tiring ourselves

For a seat

At tables

Where we aren't wanted.

Why do we feel the need to do it all

Letting Go/Uprooting

I gained control

When I realized

That my ability to blossom

Was solely

Dependent on my own energy

And the the shifting

Of my own

Paradigm.

Interlude

She was always too much for those who

Could not understand.

She found herself competing in circles.

Defined by numbers.

Numbers and graphs

And predictions.

She was liberated when she realized that her life

Was her own

Fluid

Subject

And open

To and for change.

Writing Healed Me

Self Care is not just restrained to bath bombs and therapeutic candles infused with natural oils. It's the wild unwavering and unconditional love for one's self. While struggling in this movement that some have tried to label as "The New Civil Rights Movement", I have found that love and words have lifted me. Words more than anything. Words have the ability of making us feel things that we would have never imagined. The aching of our spine while reading gruesome letters and memoirs of jailed activists, caged by society with targets on their backs.

In times when I was at my lowest, and ashamed of my anxiety, I wrote words. I spoke words. I've watched as my affirmations, both negative and positive have been manifested in the universe. Those words that rolled from my head, off my lips, and into undefined and unknown space is what made me.

Self Care also looks like being consciously aware of the

smaller universe that revolves around each of us, individually.

Where we may not have full control, but everything is

interconnected to the circulation of our energy.

Promise

In days to come

Promise me

That you will not let

America

And the patriarchy

Sweep over

And intentionally forget

The work and labor of young, black women.

Promise me that you will not let the success

And the potential of the success

Of a man

Hinder us from moving forward

And taking the first step.

Don't put us on trial and attempt to find us guilty of passion.

It is undeniable.

Do not criminalize our love

And strength.

For we have endured and continue to endure the things

That your privilege will not allow you to conceptualize.

Sweet November

My November was when the air was thick

The swing on the porch creaking back and forth

Yvonne would tell me of the war and her husband who lived in

Germany

I could never fully grasp the concept of there being a world

Outside of this small town.

I knew not that there was anything beyond this block.

Where my Black neighbors were moving out,

And my white neighbors

in.

It's April now.

Here I am sitting on the beach in Malaga.

It's coming full circle.

Lonely, Not alone.

Reaching a point of solitude

May not be your lowest.

In this labor of love for justice

And peace.

Points will be belabored

Battle will reach a standstill.

But

In those periods that do not lead to big moments,

Find rest and comfort in breathing

And reconnecting

With yourself.

Matriarch.

She is her brother's keeper

And her mother's confidant.

The world continues to crash on her shoulders

While her energy is constant.

She saves you from catastrophe just by

The tapping of her feet

The swinging of her hips

And the nodding of her head.

You find refuge in her eyes

As she shields you with her breasts.

To the Overthinker

Thinking things by as opportunities pass.

Weaving in and out of fantasies and

A few realities.

Struggling with the idea of transition.

My intuition tells me when it's truly time.

Monday Mantra

Slow down

Smell the coffee

Have the tea

Recite the Affirmation.

Black Lives Matter.

(Repeat)

No one will quite understand the feeling of standing

On the front lines

Until they have done just that.

There is nothing more powerful

Than taking a stand

In love

Hand in hand

Because of love

Against everyone

And everything

That is organized against you

Structured to hate you

And would do anything to see you destroyed.

A Message for Healing.

Stop touching your wounds to see if they've healed.

You're only stopping yourself from growing.

The person or thing that caused your pain,

Has already moved on.

All that I am,

All that I will ever be,

I have learned that I can never be a piece of myself

Without being all of me.

Ghana.

May 2018.

Unpopular.

Everytime you take a stand,

You won't be applauded.

You might even be told to sit down, instead.

Be not shaken or moved,

By others' fear of progress and uncomfortable change.

And even when

They try to convince you that you aren't enough

Rest in knowing

That you are more than

That.

these walls could recite

You would hear my shouts.

You would know just how many times my battle with identity

Has brought me to my knees

Fearing that tomorrow might not ever come.

I look around

And I wonder

Is the sun really shining

If there is no justice?

But still

I am

Here.

III. Here

How did we get here?

I watched as the James Fields jr. verdict came in and it barely felt like Justice. Our community needs closure because we will forever be recovering from the tragedy that took place on 4th street in Charlottesville on August 12th, 2017, but those wounds go much deeper; I found this once I took a look at my own family.

I sat in my aunt's office during lunch one day, and asked for what felt like the hundredth time, "how is Aunt Jeanette my aunt?" I expected a story of how my grandmother and Jeanette had become great friends over the years, and Jeanette just called herself my aunt. What I got instead was a powerful narrative of liberation; a story of how black women championed the cause of Black education in Charlottesville through community, family, and home. They never lived to see their justice beyond integration; so, I write this for my great-grandmother, Thelma, a light and unsung pioneer of Charlottesville's journey to equal access to education for students of color. I write this for my extended family to whom I became kin through a labor of love, a fight to attend school.

I thought my moment of realization had hit when George Zimmerman was found not guilty for the brutal murder of Trayvon Martin. I was angry, fired up, and ready for action. Then, I authored the petition calling for the removal of the Lee Statue and renaming of Lee Park in downtown Charlottesville; it turns out that was my moment. My moment of realization came when during my time of erasure. The moments when my words were being quoted without being credited to me, when my single act was being amplified without any sign of myself; that was when my moment came. But I am only a single story. Black women/femmes have been erased from their own movements for decades. In the case of Charlottesville, it turns out that it happens more often than not.

My great-grandmother Thelma was a freedom fighter, in every way. Her thirst for educational justice led to her two sons being two of the first twelve students to integrate schools in Charlottesville, Virginia. I carry her fire and passion with me, today as I continue to fight for equal access to higher level courses for students of color in the same school district. She used what she had to help make a change in this space, by taking in families and Black Students into her home so that they could attend the local Black School. Now, they are all family. This place meant something to her, just as it does to me. Everyone in 10th and Page knew my grandmother, and they her words meant a lot to many. From the many conversations she had on the front porch of her house on Anderson Street, or the many meetings she held in her living room; she was invested in this community.

I'm thankful for her diligence, and the work of many others who she joined in the fight for educational equity. I know that I am where I am because of her. Her spirit has trickled down

and brought me to where I am now. Like Thelma, in all that I do,

and for every door that opens, I plan to bring others along. My

hope is not to enter as one, but to enter as many.

Over the past 365 segments of time

I realized

That time neither

Comes

Nor goes.

Time does not heal

Especially not souls,

If it did

We might not be still spinning in this circular motion of

Depression

Oppression

And Regression.

Keep your eyes on your own paper.

Love your thoughts.

Only compare yourself to

The yesterday version of you.

Within seven days,

Day and night was created.

Our interpretation followed with the rising and falling of the sun,

And the inception

And fruition

Of our own ideas.

Perhaps,

The paradox of light and darkness

Is equity

For the world.

Two worlds rather,

That exist respectively

And turn

Interchangeably.

Gunned Down/Unarmed

Standing for freedom.

And for the human

Who will never be the first love

Of their unborn child.

Where this flower blooms

There is beauty in shortcomings.

No real expectation to be perfect,

Blooming in the trenches,

That's above average after all.

Surviving.

There are different seasons in life.

a season for rest

a season for growth and advancement.

And a season for seizing the unknown.

The trick to it all is being able to decipher those seasons

When they are right in front of us.

Put yourself in spaces that have space for flourishing.

Take care of yourself.

Make time for yourself.

Admire yourself.

Rest.

Discernment

We outgrow things

And people.

We must not feel obligated to

Oblige.

Always.

Protect your space

Preserve your work

Conserve Your Energy.

Life is too short to limit your own thinking

and way of living

based on the guilt

And fragility of those who have utilized privilege

To stifle your speech.

Ground yourself in what you believe in.

Stand strong.

You will not be silenced.

What greater love exists than the love that is the driving force behind protecting the liberties, rights, and lives of our neighbors? Perhaps, we are where we are now because of a lack of love for each other and what we believe in. A lack of love for equity. A lack of love for those whose skin is a different color than our own. An absence of love for the fluidity of sexuality.

We must labor in our love.

I used to lack flexibility in my imagination

My need for practicality closed my mind to the

Unpredictable

Unrealistic

World

That existed beyond the boundaries of division and injustice.

I wish that at a younger age

Someone would have told me

That I am better than

My worst day.

I wish that someone had told me that

My competitive spirit

And energy was being used

In a way that would ultimately

Lead to a desire for self destruction.

I wish someone told me early on

That there would be battles that are too

Heavy for me.

Because now,

These battles are a part of me.

Instead of just telling Black Women

To go off and tell their own stories,

Use your platform

To tell the *truth*.

Amplify Black women

Because we've been overshadowed enough.

Zion.

I dream of a time in black feminism

When we can worry about the struggles of the black woman

Without having to be told that we are contributing to the

struggles of the Black man in doing so.

I wish that we could talk about the violence being done to Black

women and femmes without the fake love and deflecting.

Perhaps, another march is not what we need.

Not another rally,

But the deep internal work of *believing* women of color.

The work of not just hearing us, but *listening*.

Instead of telling us what is best for us, put your resources, time,

and energy behind Black Women.

Don't tell us what we need.

Support us.

Give us space to be vulnerable

And open.

Love us.

Journal entry.

It is important that we see white supremacy

And other forms of discrimination

For what they are.

Fragile.

Court Support.

June 2018.

You beg for me to be polite

And hold back my rage

So that you can go on with your meeting

While Black unarmed lives are *still* being stolen.

And you claim that it brings you no joy

To watch me suffer silently

Sinking

Pressing

Gasping for air

Yet, you turn the other way.

Black girl finds refuge in the "Biographies" section of the Library.

You can find her on the far right-bottom corner

Of the bookshelf.

Adjacent to the outlet for her phone charger,

There she is submerged in the world of black revolutionaries.

Her soul is being filled,

While her vessel that connects her to the rest of the world is

being refueled.

Your anti-racist

And anti-fascist "work"

Doesn't work

If you're also homophobic.

Breathe.

And remember that

Deplatforming works.

grounding.

In those moments

Where the world is whirling.

Care for your roots.

Plant yourself deeply in what you know.

Reaching a point of solitude
Is not your lowest.
In this work,
Points will be belabored.

You will feel like you have reached a standstill.
In those periods that do not lead to big moments,
Find rest and peace in breathing
And reconnecting with yourself.

But, she too needs time to regroup.
She needs breaks from all of the burden.
That's when solidarity steps in.

Be vigilant enough
To be empowered for yourself-
Not in a way that is self-destructive
Or ultimately oppressive.

The concept of power is not the only thing
Standing between you and your liberation.
But it's also a closed mind
That is not willing to learn
And grow.

And in this dark skin
My confidence is the result of
Tears
Joy
And sadness.
Your skewed vision of my worth
Will never grant you the power
To take this away.

Even after each route has been weighed,
At the end of the day
You can say no.
Stand firm in that.

Your passion is what makes you.
Don't change.
They don't have to understand it.

Just because it is not your
Experience
Does not mean that it is not
An experience
That exists.

There are deeply rooted
Systems
All working together
To keep us
In our place.
TAKE THEM ALL DOWN.

intersectionality.

Being socially conscious
Does not give you a pass
To exploit people of other marginalized identities.

This is our story to tell.
Oh, how we will tell of our triumph.
We built this.

And when the sun comes
And the mourning clears
May we keep our outrage.
May we never lose sight of the ugly piercing screams
That follow
The brutalizing of
Our beautiful beings.
We cannot forget.

We cannot forget the ones we've lost.
Say their names.

A dream

No walls.
No borders.
No prisons.
No silence.

A Call to Action

If you are new to this work, put your resources behind the people of color who have already been doing the work.
Pay Black Women.
Cite Black Women.
Love Black Women.
Believe Black Women.
Follow Black Women.

We can and always will lead the way.

Thank You for Staying
This is The Outro.

These words have traveled into this collection from torn journals that have lived as vagabonds in my backpacks and purses traversing borders all over the country. Some finished, and some of which I've never visited the last page. What I do know is that, these are the things that got me out of bed on the days when being a Black girl landed me in a state of defeatism. Those days when my unpopular role as a local activist led to missed opportunities and closed doors. Those moments when I had to choose my conscience over the ways of the world that told me that I was fine with the way that things were. Complacency.

Over and over again, we have seen that when the youth are strong and well supported, the entire community does well. I plan to continue to advocate for a quality education for students of color and people who identify as being low-income, by identifying alternative methods of tracking academic progress

that is not discriminatory. While mentoring the middle school girls

that I currently mentor, I have come to realize how imperative it is

that I pass the things that I have learned along to others. With this

in mind, I hope to connect more students to the resources that I

have found by helping introduce students like myself to key

decision-making spaces.

I will keep planting seeds so that the impact of the

seeds that were planted in me continue to manifest.

This collection is for the child who had no real idea of

who they were until they experienced a random epiphany that

was evoked by a tweet posted on Instagram in the thick of the

summer. For the girl who played with me when I was small and

taught me about her traditions and her family that she had to

leave back in El Salvador. Just as much as it is for the people who

told me to talk less and control my thoughts because they

believed that there was a time and place for the trauma that black people have to deal with on a daily basis. For those that often spoke of this space that existed for me to be angry, but they did everything in their power to simultaneously destroy that space until there was no longer one. control, bondage, and civility over the Liberation of the individual and collective body. This collection has been a part of my healing, and thus, I hope helps someone else along their journey. I wrote the things we have been feeling for so long. My prayer is that while we all push ourselves to keep fighting, that we also find and preserve our peace.

Love and Solidarity,

Zy Bryant

We can do this.

I love us.

We keep us safe.

REFLECT.

Zyahna Bryant, is an award-winning student activist and community organizer. In the Spring of 2016, Zyahna wrote the petition calling for the removal of Confederate statues from Charlottesville's parks, and City Council voted to remove them in 2017. She continues to lead the conversation locally and nationally about race, space, and confederate monuments while organizing with local teens and youth leaders around issues of race and inequity. Her primary focus remains on how racial landscapes contribute to the achievement gap and educational inequity on a regional and national scale. Zyahna has been featured in *The New York Times, National Geographic, The New Yorker Magazine, Forbes; and featured on Vice News, PBS, CNN, and BET.*

For more information, visit Zybryant.com